Animals of the Night

Shari Last

As evening falls, the sun goes down
and blue sky fades to black.
Some creatures have been hunting all day –
they're tired and they turn back.

They scurry, wriggle, and nestle
into their lairs, and nests, and dens.
They go bed – those sleepyheads –
snuggling with their friends.

Out comes the moon with its white glow,
and proudly shines so bright.
But not everyone's asleep right now...
because some creatures come out at night.

Fluttering from flower to flower,
moths drink nectar sweet,

While fireflies glow, above and below,
in the heavy summer heat.

With super sharp ears, foxes listen for prey that they can't see.

Owls hoot while hedgehogs scurry, sniffing out their prey.

Moles pop out of their holes at night,
then sleep in them all day.

Rats find food to nibble on and trash to build their nests.

Bats awaken in their caves, then fly to catch insects!

Raccoon families find tasty treats by scavenging in bins.

Skunks leave stinky
scents behind,
blowing on the wind.

Sugar-glider clans gather in tree hollows where they nest.

Sloths stay still most of the time.
It's called active rest.

Mosquitos hum and buzz at night, seeking their next meal.

Cockroaches creep from cracks and rocks, using their antennae to feel.

Leopards hunt in silence,
piercing the darkness with sharp eyes.

They carry food up into trees,
so their rivals won't realize.

Catfish use their whiskers to hunt for food at night.

Eels slink out of coral caves and give their prey a fright!

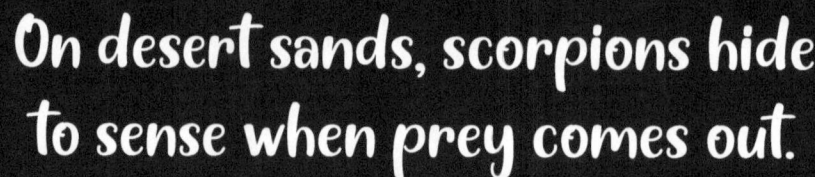

On desert sands, scorpions hide
to sense when prey comes out.

A pangolin forages for tasty bugs, digging with its snout.

And when the nighttime turns to dawn, the sun spreads its warm light.

These nocturnal creatures head to bed after their busy night!

First published in Great Britain in 2024
by TELL ME MORE Books

Text copyright ©2024 Shari Last
Design copyright ©2024 Shari Last

ISBN: 978-1-917200-42-4

Picture credits: Thanks to baddesigner.

All rights reserved. Without limiting the rights under the copyright reserved above, no part of this publication may be reproduced, stored in, or introduced into a retrieval system, or transmitted, in any form, or by any means (electronic, mechanical, photocopying, recording or otherwise), without the prior written permission of the copyright owner.

WWW.TELLMEMOREBOOKS.COM